POLTERGEISTS

OPPOSING VIEWPOINTS®

Look for these and other exciting *Great Mysteries:*

GREAT MYSTERIES

POLTERGEISTS

OPPOSING VIEWPOINTS®

by Peter & Connie Roop

Greenhaven Press, Inc.　　San Diego, California

Book design by Joan Gordon, Minneapolis
Cover design by FAB Artists, Minneapolis

Library of Congress Cataloging-in-Publication Data

Roop, Peter.
    Poltergeists.

    (Great mysteries)
    Bibliography: p.
    Includes index.
    Summary: Describes the characteristics of poltergeists and their behavior and examines the controversy surrounding their existence.
    1. Poltergeists—Juvenile literature.
[1. Poltergeists]   I. Roop, Connie.   II. Title.
III. Series: Great mysteries (Saint Paul, Minn.)
BF1483.R66   1987   133.1'4   87-8392
ISBN 0-89908-052-9 (lib. bdg.)

For Connie, who was the "ghostwriter" on this one.

Contents

"When men and women lose the sense of mystery, life will prove to be a gray and dreary business, only with difficulty to be endured."
          Harold T. Wilkins, author of Strange Mysteries
          of Time and Space

Introduction

"Penetrating so many secrets, we cease to believe in the unknowable. But there it sits nevertheless, calmly licking its chops."

H.L. Mencken, American essayist

This book is written for the curious—those who enjoy the hunt for possible solutions to the unexplained.

Mysteries are everywhere. To be human is to be constantly surrounded by wonderment. How do birds fly? Are ghosts real? How sophisticated is animal communication? How did the first baker discover how to make bread? Why are there no more dodo birds? Was King Arthur real or a fiction? Where did the world come from? Where is it going?

Great Mysteries: Opposing Viewpoints books are intended to offer the reader an opportunity to explore some of the many mysteries that both trouble and intrigue us. For the span of each book, we want the reader to feel that he or she *is* a scientist exploring the extinction of the dinosaur, an archaeologist exploring the origins of the great Egyptian pyramids, a psychic detective exploring the existence of magic.

One thing all mysteries have in common is that there is no ready answer. Often there are *many* answers but none on which even the majority of authorities agrees. *Great Mysteries: Opposing Viewpoints* books introduce the intriguing views of the experts, allowing the reader to participate in their explorations, their theories, and their disagreements as they try to explain the mysteries of our world.

But most readers won't want to stop here. *Great Mysteries: Opposing Viewpoints* aim to stimulate the reader's curiosity. Although truth is often impossible to discover, the search is fascinating. It is up to the reader to examine the evidence, to decide whether the answer is there—or to explore further.

9

One

Meeting a Poltergeist

"What was that?" Mark Miller asked.

"What was what, dear?" asked his wife Sarah.

"That noise. It sounded like someone throwing rocks against the house."

"I didn't hear anything," Mrs. Miller replied.

Mr. Miller looked out the living room window. The streetlight in front of the house lit the lawn and the newly spaded garden. Mr. Miller didn't see anyone. He did, however, notice a flat rock filling the hole he had dug that afternoon. Puzzled, he returned to his chair and picked up his newspaper.

A half hour later Mr. Miller heard four loud thuds, this time at the front door.

"I heard it this time!" exclaimed Mrs. Miller.

Mr. Miller ran to the door and flung it open. No one was there. He bent down to pick up four pebbles from the front

step. The stones felt strangely warm.

"It's probably just one of Mary's friends playing a trick," suggested Mrs. Miller.

"If I catch him, I'll show him a trick or two," threatened Mr. Miller. "He might break a window or hurt someone with his fooling around."

Just then Mary, who had recently turned thirteen, came running downstairs.

"Mother, Daddy," she cried. "Something's upstairs. I heard this loud knocking in my room." Mary began sobbing.

While Mrs. Miller comforted her daughter, Mr. Miller went upstairs.

"I couldn't find anything," he said angrily when he returned to the living room. "Mary, is this some sort of trick?"

Before Mary could answer, the lights in the hall flickered off and on three times.

❝All argument is against ghosts, but all belief is for them."

18th-century wit Samuel Johnson

The Millers looked at each other in amazement.

Suddenly a chair in the living room rose several inches off the floor and moved towards Mary. Mr. Miller grabbed it and felt it vibrating. All at once it dropped back down.

"What in the world is going on?" exclaimed Mrs. Miller.

The Millers didn't know it yet, but they had just met a poltergeist.

What Is a Poltergeist?

The Millers and the strange events in their house are entirely fictional. However, this story contains many of the elements found in classic poltergeist experiences: furniture moving on its own, flying stones, strange knockings, and lights mysteriously turning off and on. And while the Millers' poltergeist case is fictional, claims are made that many visitations of mischievous poltergeists are real.

Poltergeist is the German word for "noisy ghost" or

Rocks mysteriously fly at windows as servants watch in alarm. St. Quentin, France, 1849.

"racketing spirit." It comes from the German *polter*, suggesting racket or clatter, and *geist*, or ghost.

Recorded stories of poltergeists go back to the early days of Christianity. Bishop Germanus of France reported one of the earliest poltergeists around 450 AD. He described "walls pelted with a shower of stones." The bishop claimed they were thrown by two unburied dead men who were haunting the house in which he was staying.

Over the last 1,500 years, poltergeist reports have continued and increased. Poltergeists have visited most countries around the world—Italy, France, Germany, Britain, Iceland, the United States, South Africa, the USSR, and many others.

Most ghosts make visible appearances, but poltergeists are rarely seen. They do, however, cause startling visual effects: Drops of blood ooze from paintings; ghostly, disembodied arms and fingers appear; misshapen creatures loom into view and then disappear; eerie lights flicker on and off in unoccupied rooms.

Most poltergeists announce their presence by doing tricks. They lift, slap, push, and even pinch their victims. Some specialize in causing objects to move mysteriously. Furniture dances wildly, beds levitate, fruits and nuts drop from thin air. Throwing dishes, pans, and vases is another favorite poltergeist activity. One poltergeist dropped dead lizards and frogs on a shocked English family while they

Blood oozes from pictures, and disembodied limbs float in the air.

Poltergeists disrupt a home in Guillonville, France, 1849.

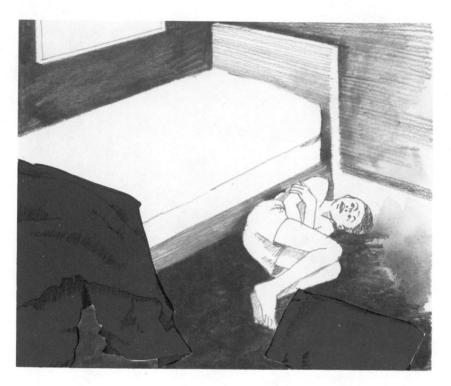

Poltergeists sometimes steal the bedcovers and throw the shivering victims to the floor.

were eating dinner. Kidney beans showered another bewildered family. Rocks, gravel, sticks, and knives are other poltergeist playthings.

Poltergeists are best known, however, for rapping, scratching, and tapping. Some scratch doors; others scrape beds. Some pound on doors; others "bounce" balls down stairs. Many rattle windows. All are bothersome.

Poltergeists make human-sounding noises like screaming, moaning, and panting. Poltergeists imitate doors unlatching, footsteps dragging, skirts swishing, and bells ringing.

Some poltergeists taunt their victims by ripping off blankets and sheets in the night and then rudely dumping their shivering victims onto the floor. Some pinch a victim's arms, legs, even buttocks. Some wrestle humans to the floor and pin them there. Poltergeists hold doors tightly shut and then open them when least expected.

A few poltergeists are fascinated with money. They shower their victims with invisible coins that feel like real money. Other cause money to appear, then disappear. One conscientious poltergeist even left change after "borrowing" some money.

Poltergeists are blamed for all of these actions and activities. Yet a question remains: Do poltergeists actually exist? Many people claim they are real, but many others dismiss them as pure fantasy or outright trickery. Whether fiction or fact, poltergeists continue to fascinate people around the world.

Two

Tracking the Elusive Poltergeist

Reports of poltergeists share one basic similarity: They concentrate on boys and girls just reaching puberty, often a time of physical and emotional stress.

William G. Roll, project director of the Psychical Research Foundation and a leading American poltergeist expert, evaluated 116 poltergeist cases and found that 92 cases focused on a particular family member or members. This "focus person" was most often between 13 and 14 years old.

Author and poltergeist-believer David Knight writes, "Often such 'poltergeist boys and girls,' as they are called, are undergoing deep-seated emotional stresses connected with developing sexual energies. Investigators now think that this inner mental stress may somehow transfer itself outside the body and in some unknown way cause the poltergeist manifestations." In other words, a poltergeist may not be a

" *In a majority of cases, the person around whom the poltergeist seems to be centered is a child or young person."*

Author Jose Feda, Mind Over Matter

separate beings; it may be a kind of *extension* of an individual.

Many poltergeist researchers believe that poltergeists are a paranormal phenomenon. Paranormal phenomena are sometimes called *psi* for *psychical*. They are real or supposed events that have no clear scientific explanation. One example is extrasensory perception, the ability to sense things in ways other than the usual seeing or hearing. People who research paranormal phenomena are called parapsychologists. Another commonly used term for paranormal research is psychical research. The intent of psychical research is to collect and analyze evidence of paranormal phenomena scientifically in order to prove whether or not they are genuine.

> **❝** *Since. . . trickery has been found applicable in some well-known cases, some writers have shown a tendency to explain all cases of poltergeist-haunted children by a 'naughty little girl' theory."*
>
> Author A.R.G. Owen, Can We Explain the Poltergeist?

Scientists and psychical researchers are deeply interested in the poltergeist's ability to transport or move objects. To discover clues about this power, they study "psychokinesis," or PK. This is the ability to move things with the mind rather than with the body—"mind over matter." *Psycho* means of the mind or soul and *kinesis* refers to the energy of motion. An example of PK would be making a cassette tape float in the air without physically moving it.

Many PK claims have been made, but few—if any—have been proven. Still, many such claims have been tested, and many psychical researchers say the test results support the existence of PK.

Skeptical scientists, however, often successfully challenge this. One respected skeptic, magician James Randi, even goes so far as to offer a $10,000 reward to anyone who can perform any paranormal feat under laboratory conditions. Randi's criteria for proof include video and tape recordings of a feat. Of the 600 applicants for the reward, not one of

Irma Schrey was the focus person of the poltergeist activity in the Schrey household in Germany. One of several frightening events was the mysterious cutting of Irma's thick braids. One day, as she carried firewood into the family kitchen, her left braid simply fell into the basket even though no visible hand had come near her. The girl's mother wrapped Irma's head in a towel, but soon both the towel and the second braid were cut off.

the people who claim to have paranormal skills (including PK abilities) has been able to demonstrate them beyond a doubt.

Randi and many other scientists believe that in order to prove the actual existence of poltergeists, the poltergeist phenomena must be duplicated under strict laboratory conditions. Until concrete examples of poltergeist phenomena can be suitably demonstrated and studied, questions will remain.

Testing Poltergeists

The branch of psychokinesis most interesting to poltergeist researchers is "recurrent spontaneous psychokinesis," or RSPK. This means that objects move without visible cause repeatedly and uncontrollably over a period of time. Poltergeist phenomena are classified as RSPK because they appear to recur without their victims being able to control them, even though victims may be causing them.

A person gifted with PK should be able to move objects in a controlled environment. This is critical in judging poltergeist phenomena because few, if any, poltergeist-caused activities (like rapping) are repeated when scientific conditions are present. Poltergeists and their focus persons don't seem to want to perform in laboratories.

The questions remain. Are poltergeists real? Are focus persons with PK skills the real poltergeists, their invisible energies released in times of emotional and physical stress? Or are poltergeist happenings just elaborate hoaxes perpetrated for attention?

An examination of four well-known and documented poltergeist cases might provide insights, if not answers, about this mystery.

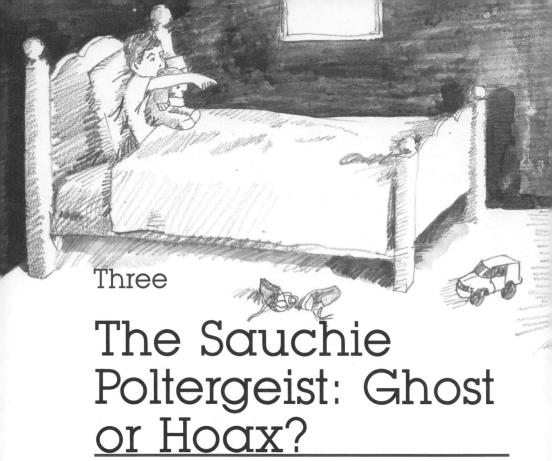

Three

The Sauchie Poltergeist: Ghost or Hoax?

The evening of November 22, 1960, began quietly in the
house of Mr. Thomas Campbell of Sauchie, Scotland. But this
peace was soon to be disturbed by one of the most puzzling
poltergeists ever reported.

That night the two Campbell children, six-year-old Derek
and nine-year-old Margaret, went to bed at their regular
time. Their eleven-year-old cousin Virginia, who was living
with them temporarily, joined them in their room. Margaret
and Virginia shared a bed. This disturbed Virginia, who was
used to a bed of her own.

After the girls went to bed, a loud thunking noise was
heard. It sounded like a bouncing ball. The girls, surprised
and puzzled, searched their room, then went downstairs to
Mrs. and Mr. Campbell who were in the living room. The
thunking noise followed them. As Mr. Campbell searched for
the source of the strange sound, the noise continued. After a

while the girls went nervously back to bed. Only when Virginia was asleep did the mysterious noise stop.

Virginia stayed home from school the next day. At tea time she was sitting in the living room with Mr. and Mrs. Campbell. Suddenly the large, heavy sideboard against the wall moved five inches out from it, then back. Amazed, the Campbells and Virginia watched. No one had touched it.

That night Virginia went to bed alone. After the strange experiences of the past two days, the Campbells thought she might sleep better if she slept by herself. She was still awake when the thunking sounds returned. This time they could be heard all over the house. Several neighbors were called in to witness the unusual noises.

More Poltergeist Tricks

One neighbor brought the Reverend Mr. Lund, the minister of the church where Virginia went to Sunday School. Mr. Lund heard the knocking noise as soon as he entered the house. He joined eight other witnesses. According to Lund, all this adult attention did not seem to excite Virginia.

He pinpointed the knocking noise. It came from the head of Virginia's bed. Suspecting a trick, Reverend Lund told Virginia to move so she could not possibly hit the headboard with her head. He checked to see that her feet were tightly tucked under the covers. The knocking continued. Lund grabbed the head of the bed with both hands. He felt it vibrate in time with the knockings. He again checked Virginia and the bed for tricks, but could not find the source of the noise.

Then suddenly a fifty-pound linen chest near the end of the bed began rocking. The chest rose in the air, moved almost two feet across the floor, then moved back. Mr. Lund put his hand on it, and it settled back down onto the floor.

Virginia was scared. She could no longer lie still in bed. The adults present were also becoming upset. To ease the tension, Lund joked with Virginia that it was her boyfriend knocking for her and that she should knock back. Everyone laughed at his joke and relaxed a little.

Mr. Lund told Margaret to get into bed with Virginia. There was a immediate outburst of knocking. When

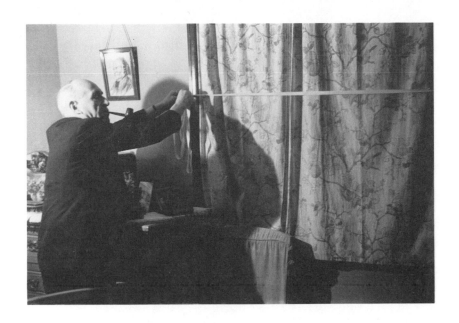

Investigating poltergeists: Top: Famous ghost-hunter Harry Price seals a window to test for a poltergeist in England. Right: A police officer in Baden, Germany coats a doorknob with a special chemical that will blacken the hands of any human touching it.

Margaret bravely climbed into bed, the knocking grew violent, almost as if it resented her presence. Margaret quickly left. Gradually, Virgina calmed down and finally slept. The knocking stopped.

The next morning Reverend Lund telephoned Dr. Nisbet, the family physician. Lund's story of the strange knockings surprised Nisbet. Curious, he agreed to join Lund that evening for a personal investigation. The two men also invited another doctor, Dr. Gordon, and another minister, the Reverend Mr. Manson.

66 *It seemed as though the rappings and the trances might be alternative outlets for the suppressed emotions of a girl transplanted from her accustomed environment, and subjected to the stresses of an early adolescence."*
Authors Alan Gauld and A.D. Cornell, Poltergeists: Hauntings and the Haunted

The Campbells told Lund and his companions that the knockings had occurred again. So as not to upset Virginia unnecessarily, Lund went alone to see her. While he watched, Virginia's pillow began turning under her head. The pillow slowly shifted sixty degrees. Virginia was visibly upset.

Nisbet, Gordon, and Manson joined Lund and Virginia. In order to prevent a trick of any sort, the men asked Virginia to lie on top of the covers where they could watch her movements. Nothing unusual happened while the men watched.

After an uneventful hour or so, all the men except Mr. Lund left. He heard the knocking again and saw the chest move slightly. Mr. Campbell told Lund that earlier, when Virginia had been close to the chest, it has "knocked back at her."

Virginia went back to school the next afternoon. Her teacher, Miss Stewart, had not heard about the strange events. When Mr. Hill, the headmaster, told Miss Stewart that Virginia had a poltergeist, Miss Stewart thought it was an illness. She was totally unprepared for the events that would happen in her classroom.

At two-thirty that afternoon, the children were reading silently at their desks. Miss Stewart was busy correcting papers. Occasionally she checked to see that everyone was reading. Once when she looked up, she noticed that the lid of Virginia's desk was moving slowly up and down. The desk top rose about forty-five degrees and gently went back down. None of the children sitting near Virginia were aware of it.

Was It a Joke?

At first, Miss Stewart thought Virginia was opening her desk to get something. She was about to reprimand her when she saw that Virginia was actually trying to hold down the desk top with both hands. Suspecting a joke, Miss Stewart checked to see if Virginia was moving the desk with her legs. Virginia had both feet squarely on the floor and was sitting normally. Miss Stewart stared at Virginia in silent reproach. Virginia silently stared back, a worried look in her eyes.

> **66** *Another piece of conventional wisdom is that the poltergeist is the product of unhappiness, guilt or sexual frustration, particularly in adolescent children, a release of emotion converted into a playful force which can move objects or disrupt households. No one, however, has suggested a mechanism by which this might come about."*
>
> Authors John Fairley and Simon Welfare, Arthur C. Clarke's World of Strange Powers

Fifteen minutes later Virginia asked for permission to get a new book from the class library shelf. Miss Stewart said yes, and Virginia went to get the book. Suddenly, the empty desk behind Virginia's rose about an inch off the floor, then

How much mischief was done by "Wee Hughie" and how much by the children?

settled back down. The desk was now out of line with the other desks in the row. Miss Stewart quickly went to check the desk for strings and was surprised when she found no signs of trickery.

That evening Dr. Nisbet kept watch in Virginia's room until she went to sleep. This time, the disturbances came in cycles. First the pillow and bedclothes would move, then the knockings would be heard. Next the linen chest would move. After a period of quiet the same things happened again. Dr. Nisbet saw the pillow move as much as ninety degrees at times. The bedclothes and pillow puckered as if pulled by an invisible hand. The chest moved, its lid opening and closing.

"Wee Hughie"

At first, Virginia, Derek, and Margaret found the poltergeist activity frightening. Soon, however, they got over their fear and even took to calling the poltergeist "Wee Hughie."

Wee Hughie was blamed for pulling on the children's clothes or for causing candy to "disappear." Wee Hughie wrote on Virginia and Margaret's faces. Twice he unscrewed the stoppers from hot water bottles, soaking the girls' beds. But as these events were not seen by anyone other than the children, they were thought to be tricks.

On Monday, November 28, the poltergeist again went into action at school.

Virginia's desk mysteriously moves as does the chalkboard pointer. Was it a poltergeist at work?

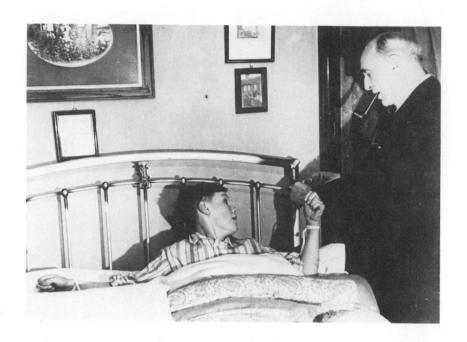

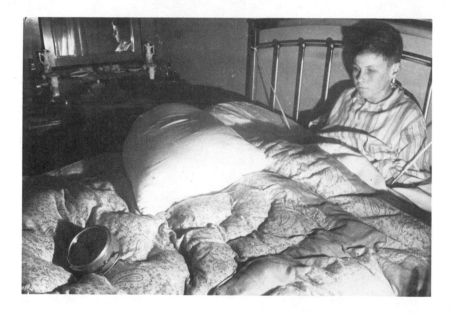

Near Crawley, England, a young boy seemed to be haunted by a poltergeist. Top: Investigator Harry Price ties the boy's hands to the bed so that it is impossible for him to reach objects and throw them. Bottom: Despite the restraints, an alarm clock from the boy's dresser mysteriously flies across the room and lands on the bed.

About ten-fifteen that morning Virginia went to Miss Stewart for help on a math problem. The rest of the class was working quietly. Virginia, her hands behind her back, stood to the left of her teacher's chair. As Miss Stewart explained the problem, the blackboard pointer on her desk began vibrating. The pointer rolled across the desk top and fell off. Miss Stewart put her hand on the desk and felt it vibrating. The desk began to move away from Virginia, rotating at an angle.

Virginia began crying, "Please, Miss, I'm not trying to do it."

Miss Stewart, trying to calm Virginia, replied, "It's all right; help me straighten the desk up." No one else noticed that anything unusual had happened.

In order to soothe Virginia, Dr. Nisbet decided it would be best to send her to Dollar, the village where her mother was living. The poltergeist followed. Unusually loud knockings were heard that evening in her mother's home.

On Tuesday, November 29, Dr. William Logan (Nisbet's partner) and his wife Sheila, who was also a doctor, visited Virginia in Dollar. They heard several outbursts of knockings ranging from gentle tappings to violent poundings. All the sounds came from near Virginia. Dr. Sheila Logan, who had been extremely skeptical about the knockings, became convinced they came from within the room and that nobody in the room had caused them.

Virginia returned to the Campbell house the next day. Nothing unusual happened that night.

On Thursday, December 1, Dr. William Logan and Dr. Nisbet set up a movie camera and a tape recorder in Virginia's bedroom. Virginia went to bed at 9:00 PM.

From then until about ten-thirty there were continuous noises, ranging from what Logan described as "agitated and demanding" knockings to rappings he could barely hear. Logan also heard some sawing sounds. Occasionally Virginia's pillow puckered and her covers rippled.

The knockings and sawing sounds were recorded by the tape recorder. The puckerings and ripplings did not last long enough for the movie camera to focus on them.

At eleven-thirty Virginia's father arrived unexpectedly from their former home. He had missed all of the troublesome events because he had been working in Ireland.

His arrival made Virginia extremely happy. It also ended the poltergeist's reign of mischief.

The poltergeist's last trick was to move a bowl of flower bulbs on Miss Stewart's desk. After that the poltergeist left Sauchie. Peace and quiet returned to the little Scottish village.

In-Depth Investigation

Dr. A.R. Owen, an experienced poltergeist investigator, heard about the Sauchie poltergeist. Curious about Virginia's experiences, he became the prime investigator of the unusual events surrounding her. Owen carefully interviewed everyone involved and came to believe firmly that the Sauchie case proved the existence of poltergeists. He wrote, "The evidence presented is, to my mind, conclusive proof of the objective reality of two types of poltergeist phenomena: production of noise (tappings, knockings, sawings, bumpings); movement of objects by paranormal means."

66 *We may see from the account given by the untrained observer of a conjuring trick how widely the thing described may differ from the thing done. . . .The conjurer induces us to adopt a wrong inference—we 'see' something which does not really take place."*

Psychical researcher Frank Podmore, The Naturalization of the Supernatural

In his book *Can We Explain the Poltergeist?* Dr. Owen argues that the eyewitness accounts in the Campbell case are strong evidence that Virginia was indeed the focus person for a poltergeist. He bases this conclusion on the testimony of the Reverend Mr. Lund, Dr. Nisbet, the two doctors Logan, and Miss Stewart. By the nature of their jobs and their academic training, Dr. Owen states, each of these responsible witnesses "may be expected to have well trained and disciplined minds."

Dr. Owen emphasizes that five different witnesses reported similar events. He says, "it is just possible in principle to suppose that one person could be the victim of illusion or hallucination. It is, however, beyond all possibility that five responsible persons should be so deceived at various occasions over a period of two weeks." He concludes that these witnesses actually saw and heard the events they reported.

“ *We cannot, for instance, suppose that in the Sauchie case of 1960, 11-year-old Virginia Campbell concealed in the fairly crowded house where she lived a sophisticated, specially made mechanism capable of rocking, lifting, dragging along, and raising the lid of a full linen chest weighing 50 pounds and that she also concealed a confederate to operate it when she was closely watched."*

Psychical researchers and authors Alan Gauld and
A.D. Cornell, Poltergeists

Could natural causes like underwater streams or old mines be to blame for the movement of the furniture and knocking noises? asked skeptics.

Dr. Owen wrote to the Surveyor's Department for information about old mines or underground streams near the Campbell house. Mr. J. Ross, Road Surveyor and Water Engineer for the county, reported to him, "To the best of our knowledge [the ground] is free from subsidence, vibration, and ground movement. There are, as far as it is known, no underground streams."

What about trickery? Was Virginia trying to gain attention by performing "poltergeist" tricks? If so, then how did she do them?

Alan Gauld and A.D. Cornell, two British poltergeist investigators, searched for evidence of trickery. They found none. In their book *Poltergeist*, they wrote, "We cannot, for instance, suppose that in the Sauchie case of 1960-61, 11-year-old Virginia Campbell concealed in the fairly crowded house where she lived a sophisticated, specially

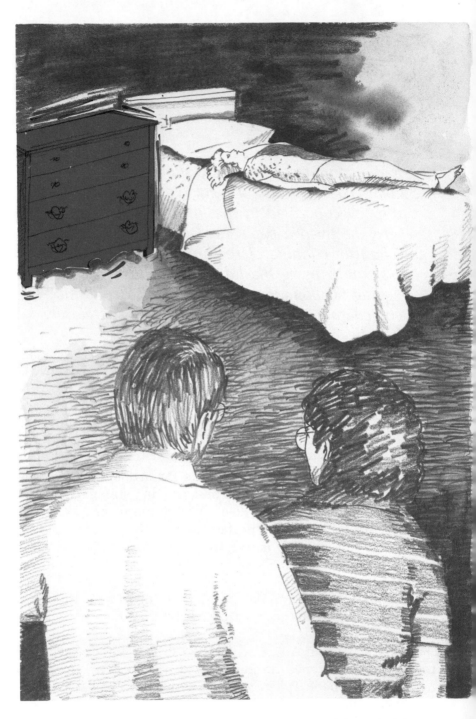

Onlookers observe Virginia as mysterious things continue to happen in the children's bedroom.

made mechanism capable of rocking, lifting, dragging along, and raising the lid of a full linen chest weighing 50 pounds, and that she also concealed a confederate to operate it when she was closely watched."

Dr. Owen also ruled out trickery. He had particularly questioned each of his witnesses to see if they had found any evidence that Virginia was playing tricks.

Miss Stewart had promptly examined the desk behind Virginia's when it moved. She found no physical cause for the movement.

Dr. Nisbet and Dr. Logan were convinced that Virginia could not have caused her pillow to pucker as her hands were not near the pillow when it happened. Reverend Lund, trying to locate the source of the knockings, had made certain that she could not hit or push the bed headboard. He had even checked that the bed was not touching the wall in case the movements came from the wall.

Dr. Logan, who had heard and recorded the sawing sounds, had tried to imitate them by drawing his fingernails across sheets and carpets. He failed.

According to Dr. Owen the reliability of the witnesses and the lack of any evidence pointing to trickery rule out Virginia's having created the poltergeist phenomena.

Was Virginia Campbell really a focus person for a poltergeist? She was a young girl entering puberty who was also undergoing a period of stress, typical attributes of a focus person.

Yet no scientific tests were done to determine if she could cause the "poltergeist" effects at will. No lab experiments were performed to see if she did indeed have the ability to move things with her mind.

Dr. Owen states, "In my opinion the Sauchie case must be regarded as establishing beyond all reasonable doubt the objective reality of some poltergeist phenomena." But many questions are still unanswered.

Why did the strange events happen only when Virginia was awake? Why did none of the other children in Virginia's class see the desk top move or the pointer fall? If Virginia and her cousins played some tricks and blamed them on Wee Hughie, then might they have done all the tricks? Why did the poltergeist leave when Virginia's father returned? The many mysteries of Sauchie remain.

Four

The Law Office Poltergeist: Fact or Fantasy?

In November, 1967, Mr. Sigmund Adam hired nineteen-year-old Annemarie Schaberl as secretary in his law office in Rosenheim, Bavaria. On the day she started work, a series of unexplained events began happening. It quickly became apparent that Annemarie Schaberl was the focus person for an unusual poltergeist.

Annemarie's effect was obvious as soon as she entered the office lobby. Overhead lamps began swinging when she walked through the halls. Light bulbs near her would suddenly burst, the glass fragments flying toward Annemarie as if attracted to her instead of falling to the floor. Fluorescent lights mysteriously went off when she was near them. Later, neon bulbs were found to be partially unscrewed in their sockets without anyone having touched them. Fuses blew without obvious electrical cause.

This poltergeist seemed fascinated with telephones. When

Attorney Sigmund Adams holds one of the telephone bills listing some of the hundreds of puzzling calls made from his office.

Annemarie was at work, the four office phones would suddenly begin ringing. Callers were often cut off in mid-conversation as the phones went dead. Phone bills soared as the number of calls increased dramatically. Arranging for only one operating phone did not stop the poltergeist's phoning. Hundreds of calls were still recorded at the telephone exchange even when no one admitted using the phone.

Mr. Adam became determined to discover what was wrong with the phones. First he had them all checked to make sure they were working correctly. Then he ordered a call-counting machine installed to monitor the number of calls made from the office, the length of each call, and what

> **❝***Parapsychologists realized long ago that most poltergeist cases are neither completely genuine nor completely phony. They are usually a mixture of both.*"
>
> *Parapsychologist D. Scott Rogo*

Professor Hans Bender: "When [Annmarie] was sent on leave, nothing happened, and when she definitely left the office for a new position no more disturbances occurred."

numbers were being called. After several weeks it became apparent that most of the phone calls went to number 0119. This number announced the correct time. The office employees denied making the calls, yet the call-counter continued to register multiple calls to the time number, sometimes as many as six a minute.

Because many of the other poltergeist pranks focused on electricity, Mr. Adam asked the Rosenheim Maintenance Department to investigate the electrical systems. A voltage amplifier, which could measure unusual surges in the power supply, was installed. Surges could explain the exploding light bulbs and blown fuses. Numerous, unexplainable surges that did not affect other buildings in the area were recorded.

> **"** *Parapsychology is a farce and a delusion, along with other claims of wonders and powers that assail us every day of our lives."*
>
> *Magician and author James Randi,* Flim-Flam! The Truth About Unicorns, Parapsychology, and Other Delusions

Above: Annemarie was bored with her job. Were the mysterious events in the office her clever way of making it more interesting? Right: Professor Hans Bender tests Annemarie's PK potential.

An emergency generator was installed to provide an even electrical flow to the office. Light bulbs still exploded.

At this point, Mr. Adam looked for other help to explain the unnerving events disturbing his office. He contacted Dr. Hans Bender, Professor of Parapsychology at the University of Freiburg, West Germany. Dr. Bender, a leading poltergeist investigator, agreed to help. In early December he and his

team of aides arrived in Rosenheim.

By detailing the times of the events and the persons present when they occurred, Bender clearly connected Annemarie Schaberl to the happenings. Intrigued by the swinging lamps, Bender's team set up a video recording unit and photographed the lamps in motion. This apparently was a historical first as no other investigators had ever succeeded in filming a poltergeist's pranks.

While Dr. Bender was in Rosenheim, a new series of poltergeist phenomena began. Startled observers watched desk drawers suddenly open and shut by themselves. Papers moved mysteriously from room to room. Pictures rocked back and forth on the walls. Paintings rotated 360 degrees before crashing to the floor. Bender's investigators videotaped one painting swinging in an arc of 120 degrees.

Annemarie took to predicting the next poltergeist activity. Once, for example, she said, "Oh, I have a strange feeling that the light bulb in the next room is going to explode!" Within moments it burst.

The Rosenheim poltergeist possessed unusual strength. Twice, while Annemarie was present, a 400-pound filing cabinet moved. Since Annemarie weighed only 95 pounds, investigators doubted she could have moved the cabinet

Was Annemarie
a victim or a
trickster?

physically even if she tried.

Clearly Annemarie Schaberl was involved in the poltergeist phenomena, but what was her role? Was she attempting to trick people and gain attention? Did Annemarie have latent PK ability that was being released? Or was she really a focus for a poltergeist?

As with similar poltergeist cases, the person most involved was a teenager under stress. Dr. Bender learned that Annemarie did not like working in the law office. She was dissatisfied and frustrated. The hours were too long, and she found the work boring. She anxiously awaited the end of each working day. She grew especially impatient toward late afternoon, continually watching the clock.

When investigators checked the times of the mysterious phone calls, they were not surprised to learn that most of them were placed at the end of the day.

Dr. Bender persuaded Annemarie to undergo a series of tests to determine her PK abilities. Under controlled laboratory conditions, she did not produce any PK manifestations. Other tests, however, revealed that Annemarie was angry and tense. She often released her anger by breaking things. Was it coincidence that the office poltergeist broke things at the times Annemarie was most frustrated?

Poltergeist supporters claim that Annemarie's unhappiness about her work was being directed against the physical furnishings of the office itself. They claim she mentally caused the strange events to happen through psychokinesis. Her mental energy *was* the poltergeist. Dr. Bender concluded that Annemarie was a poltergeist focus and ruled out any trickery on her part.

Apparently tired of the publicity, Annemarie left her job at Adam's law office. She began working for a law firm in another town. As is often the case with a focus person, the poltergeist activities followed Annemarie. This time, however, the unusual events were not publicized.

Dr. Bender reported, "When she definitely left the office for a new position, no more disturbances occurred. But similar events, less obvious and kept secret, happened for some time in the new office where she was working."

When the poltergeist phenomena at Annemarie's new office were not publicized, the poltergeist that was "haunting" Annemarie Schaberl soon departed and the unusual events stopped.

The Mystery Remains

Annemarie's case is well documented. Statements verifying the events came from scientific researchers, office personnel, electricians, and phone company officials. Physical evidence exists in photographs, videotapes, and the records of the phone counter and the voltage recorder.

Yet many questions remain. Why did the PK manifestations cease when the publicity about Annemarie did? Were the "poltergeist" phenomena a scheme by Annemarie to gain attention? Could the voltage surges be explained as accidental power increases? If Annemarie was responsible and could create the PK phenomena in the law office, why couldn't she recreate them in the lab? Did she have an accomplice at the phone company who manipulated the phone records? How was she able to predict the explosion of lightbulbs?

Something unusual happened in Rosenheim. Whether it was an actual poltergeist or a carefully planned hoax is still unresolved.

Five

The Columbus Poltergeist: Tricks or Truth?

Saturday, March 3, 1984, began quietly in the Resch home in Columbus, Ohio. The family of eight had finished their breakfast. Tina, the Resch's fourteen-year-old adopted daughter, joined the family's four foster children in the family room.

Mrs. Resch finished washing the breakfast dishes. Seeing the lights on in the empty dining room, she was puzzled and went to turn them off. She knew she had turned them off after breakfast. The lights in the hallway were back on again, too. She heard the shower upstairs running. But no one was upstairs.

Mrs. Resch went back into the kitchen because her dishwasher sounded odd. It seemed to be racing through its cycles. She stared at the clock. Its hands were whirling around wildly. Suddenly she heard loud music coming from the family room.

Electrician Claggett tapes a light switch in a vain attempt to stop the mysterious events.

Puzzled and annoyed, Mrs. Resch hurried down the hall to talk to Tina. The stereo was blaring.

"I know you told me to turn it off," Tina said, "but it just came back on."

Tina unplugged the stereo. But music still played.

Alarmed, Mrs. Resch stayed in the family room with the children until her husband returned from an errand.

Mr. Resch listened to his family explain the bizarre events. He decided to call an electrician since so many of the family's appliances seemed to have gained a mind of their own.

❝ *Once, she was sitting on the arm of a chair with her arms toward me when I saw the sofa 'attack' her."*

Photographer Fred Shannon

The electrician, Bruce Claggett, had many years of experience in dealing with electrical problems. He immediately suspected a faulty circuit breaker on the main household current. Upon checking, however, he found the switch worked perfectly.

Claggett next focused on the lights. He taped all the light switches in the house, yet even before he was done, the first lights were on again, their tape missing.

"I taped them again and again," Claggett claimed. "I went through two rolls of tape and then tried adhesive bandages."

> **"** *In one case a sofa seems to be rising in the air. . . . A close inspection of the photograph, however, clearly shows Tina's foot under the couch and apparently responsible for lifting it."*
> Paul Kurtz, A Skeptic's Handbook of Parapsychology

Growing more puzzled every moment, Claggett gathered everyone in the kitchen. He taped all four kitchen switches. "Everybody in the family was where I could see them, and no one could have touched a switch," he said. "The lights came back on."

Claggett gave up. He couldn't find the cause of the problems. "I had a strange feeling I never want to have again," Claggett stated.

Still perplexed, Claggett called the Resch home that evening to see if any solution had been found. Mr. Resch told him, "The lights seem okay now. But something worse is happening. Things are flying through the air."

Throughout the Resch house, objects were taking off. Pictures flew from their hooks. Couches rose at one end. Chairs moved. A set of glasses fell one by one from a shelf, smashing as they hit the floor.

The Resches called the police to help get to the bottom of the mystery. But the police said, "You need help, but not the kind we can give."

Exhausted from their ordeal, the Resch family stayed

together in the family room that night. Nothing unusual happened.

But early the next morning, trouble began again.

Mr. Resch was the first to connect Tina with the strange happenings. There had been an hour of peace the day before when Tina was visiting a friend. Nothing had happened Saturday night when she was asleep. And nothing unusual occurred until Tina woke up on Sunday morning.

Confronted, Tina insisted she was innocent of any trickery. "I'm not making it happen. I'm not doing it on purpose," she said.

The Resches called upon their Lutheran minister for help. He listened to their story and agreed to bless the house in hopes of ending the peculiar events. Carrying a lighted candle, he said a prayer in each room in the house.

After his departure, the disturbances began again.

At this point, Mrs. Resch decided to find other help. She called reporter Mike Harden of the *Columbus Dispatch* newspaper. Harden had written a story about the Resches and the hundreds of foster children they had cared for over the years. He agreed to come himself.

While Harden listened to Mrs. Resch's account of the events of the last two days, a cup of coffee moved and accidentally spilled into Tina's lap. Magazines began falling

In Lauter, Germany, strange sounds were heard in the Schrey family's attic. When Mrs. Schrey went upstairs, she found a carpet twisted like a snake and slithering across the floor.

off a table. Sensing a story, Harden immediately called for a photographer.

Fred Shannon, the photographer, later called it "the most bizarre assignment of my life." While at the Resch house, he saw a loveseat move towards Tina "as if to attack her." A rug rose from the floor and landed on Tina's head. Shannon claims to have seen a box of tissues take off from a table and rocket across the room. Shannon kept taking photos, hoping to catch an event in action.

A white telephone seemed to repeatedly attack Tina. Shannon tried desperately to photograph the flying phone. Nothing happened as long as he focused his camera on Tina. But as soon as he looked away, the phone took off.

Shannon was determined to outwit the camera-shy flying phone. "It was tricky, and I would have to be tricky if I were to capture it on film," Shannon said. "I decided I would outfox the force." So he readied his camera, then acted as if he was looking away from Tina. Out of the corner of his eye, he glimpsed some movement. At that moment he snapped the picture.

Shannon's camera caught the phone in full flight across Tina's body. The photograph received international attention. Other reporters, photographers, and TV crews raced to the Resches' home to get in on the story.

A series of poltergeist activities in the Plach household in Yachendorf, Germany included plates of food dumping over without being touched and household items flying through the air.

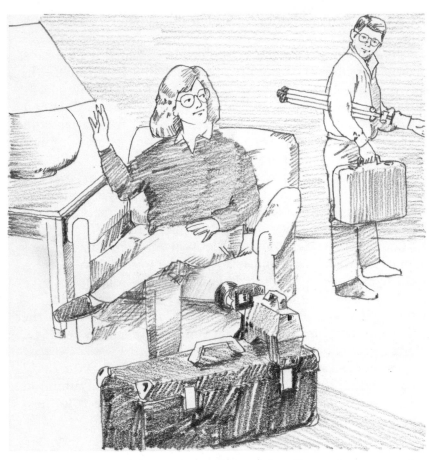

A camera is secretly left turned on and focused on Tina as the newspeople prepare to leave the Resch home.

When a reporter suggested that a poltergeist was the culprit, Mrs. Resch stated, "I don't believe in such things." She felt more comfortable calling it a "force." Asked about Tina's involvement, she said, "Maybe Tina can't control the force, but that's what it is."

One TV cameraman, however, caught the force in action.

" *The real story here, I suspect, is the reaction of a duped media. In spite of repeated efforts, I have never seen these reported events."*
Reporter David Yost

On March 8, a number of journalists had interviewed Tina, videotaping her for several news programs. One TV crew was packing up its equipment but had secretly left one camera running and focused on Tina.

Suddenly a table lamp near Tina toppled to the floor. The TV camera caught it in motion. The excited TV crew rushed back to the station to see what they had filmed. The results were surprising. Tina had been caught red-handed pulling a "poltergeist" trick.

> **❝** *There was no hoax involved. Tina's powers are frightening and I feared for her safety."*
> Photographer Fred Shannon

The film, shown in slow motion, captured what the human eye had missed—Tina quietly looking around to see if anyone was watching her, seeing the coast clear, reaching up to pull the lamp over. Her first attempt failed so she tried again. This time she succeeded in knocking the lamp over. At the same time, Tina leaped up screaming.

Confronted with this evidence of trickery, Tina explained, "I was tired and angry. I did it so the reporters could have what they came for and leave." The reporters believed her.

The family next invited a team from the Psychical Research Foundation of Chapel Hill, North Carolina, to investigate. William Roll, Director of the Foundation, came with his assistant Kelly Powers to track down the force.

Collecting Evidence

Roll, one of the foremost investigators of "poltergeist" claims, was readily admitted to the Resch home. In fact, Roll and his assistant stayed a week with the Resches, collecting evidence. They checked for natural causes but found none. They looked for wires and trick devices that could have created the effects. They found nothing. They also accepted Tina's explanation for the trick she had been caught doing.

Roll and Powers closely watched Tina. Still the events continued. Roll reported seeing a pair of pliers move five feet.

Drawings based on photographs Fred Shannon took while observing Tina and the poltergeist activities. James Randi interpreted them this way: Top left: By grasping the cord at the arrow, Tina could cause the phone to fly up into the

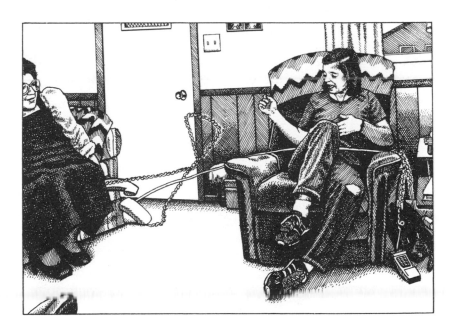

position shown in bottom left. Top right: Tina appears to have been holding the phone base and has thrown the handset out of the edge of the picture. Bottom right: A witness watches as the phone appears to fly at her.

He saw a tape recorder move, too.

To further test Tina, Roll persuaded the Resches to let Tina go to the Foundation's lab at Chapel Hill to undergo a series of tests.

Roll tested her for extrasensory perception (ESP) ability. According to Roll, Tina often knew information about people before meeting them. In one test, Tina was blindfolded and taken for a car ride. She was able to guess with unusual accuracy the colors of other cars they passed. Yet Roll's tests ultimately proved inconclusive. Before he completed his research, Tina broke her leg in a motorcycle accident. She went home to recover. Two months passed before she was up and around again, and then she was unwilling to finish the tests.

The Resch home returned to normal after Tina's accident. Things have remained calm ever since.

Challenges to Tina's Poltergeist

The Columbus poltergeist case has its serious challengers. For one thing, Tina Resch was caught playing a trick. But did this one incident disprove all the other poltergeist phenomena experienced?

A look at Tina's background and situation at the time of the events might shed more light on these experiences.

" *I have observed Tina closely and I don't believe her claims are in any way part of a hoax."*

Psychic investigator William Roll

The Resches had adopted Tina at an early age. Now that she was fourteen, Tina had become interested in finding her natural mother. The Resches tried to prevent her from doing this. Tina persisted. Stress over this situation was building.

Tina was easily upset. She was hyperactive and had been removed from school because of it. She had been privately tutored at home. She was also undergoing the normal stress of adolescent growth and change. It is apparent that Tina was either a prime poltergeist focus person or that she was an over-anxious teenager bent on creating a scene centered on herself. Did she create a "poltergeist" to ensure that attention?

A Second Investigation

During the height of the poltergeist phenomena, the *Columbus Dispatch* sent out a call for professional help. Three members of the Committee for the Scientific Investigation of Claims of the Paranormal (CSICOP) answered that call. Headed by the famous magician James Randi, the team also included two astronomers, Steve Shore and Nick Sanduleak from Case Western Reserve University in Ohio.

CSICOP is an organization established to conduct thorough investigations of paranormal activities, including

Magician James Randi: *"[Tina] was a girl looking for attention and she got it."*

poltergeist claims. Directed by philosophy professor Paul Kurtz, CSICOP includes such prominent and respected members as scientist-writers Carl Sagan, Isaac Asimov, and Stephen Gould. The scientific background and credentials of this group are extensive, and it has an outstanding reputation for exposing fraud and successfully challenging paranormal claims. Not once have CSICOP investigators found creditable evidence in support of the existence of poltergeists.

When the CSICOP team arrived in Columbus, they found Roll and Kelly of the Psychical Research Foundation already involved with the case. Mrs. Resch said that the two astronomers could enter her home but denied access to Randi. Mrs. Resch claimed that it would be "sensationalizing" the matter to allow the "magician" to become involved.

Later Randi wrote, "I did not see how she could honestly say that in view of the commotion brought about by the great number of press conferences and interviews that had taken place in the house."

Did Tina Resch cause the "poltergeist" activities?

Dr. William Roll set up laboratory experiments to test Tina's PK ability.

Denied immediate access to the events, Randi concentrated his efforts on examining the photographs and videotapes of the events.

He focused on the flying phone. One photo of it had been seen around the world. Randi examined the other thirty-five photos on the roll of film, something the other investigators had not done. There were phones in various stages of flight in each frame.

Randi found a curious thing when he examined the photograph just preceding the one that actually caught the phone in full flight. Tina had the phone cord draped across her lap. The next thing anyone knew, the phone was "flying" across her.

Flying Phone Photos

"It is the last of the flying telephones on Fred Shannon's film that really asks a great deal of our patience," Randi states. "It shows Tina Resch seated in the chair, her pointing left hand extended right across her body. The telephone cord is horizontally stretched out and the telephone handset is so far away as to be out of the frame altogether. Tina is in a stance suggestive of a major-league baseball player

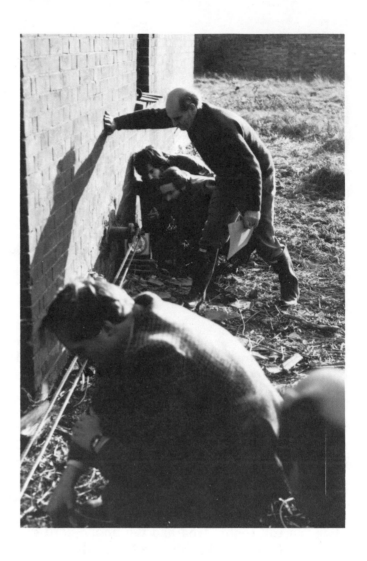

Investigating poltergeists: Poltergeist investigator Tony Cornell decided to test the "geophysical theory"—that earth movements underground might cause furniture to move, plates to fly around, and other poltergeist events to happen. With the help of engineer Scott Steedman (in the hardhat), he attached a vibrating machine to the outside of a house (top left) and another to an inside wall (top right). Bottom: Cornell and Steedman watched their instruments as the machines vibrated. They found that the noise was terrifying; dirt and plaster cascaded down; the building started to show damage. Yet nothing like "typical poltergeist phenomenon" occurred.

completing a throw to first base. We must ask ourselves if we will choose to believe that this is a photograph of a girl being affected by poltergeist activities or a photograph of a girl simply pitching a telephone across the room."

Randi's CSICOP team viewed the entire videotape of Tina's lamp-toppling trick. Later Randi was given an edited version. He was told he could not have the original. When he insisted, the TV station told him it had been accidentally erased. Randi claims that "the missing portion of the videotape showed Tina Resch carefully and obviously setting up the trick. She edged around the sofa, glancing about her to be sure she was not being observed."

Frame 20 of Fred Shannon's film also caught Tina doing the same trick. As Randi asks, "Was this one, too, 'only fooling'?"

A Hoax?

Of all the witnesses of the strange events at the Resch home, only Fred Shannon claimed that he had actually seen things take off. This corresponds with many other poltergeist cases in which things fly but no one sees them take off from their resting places. Seeing an object begin its flight would remove doubts about its having been thrown. Professor Steven Shore, Randi's co-investigator, concluded that it was all a hoax. "The hand is always quicker than the eye," he stated. The photographic evidence seems to support his conclusion.

Paul Kurtz, chairman of CSICOP, easily duplicated Tina's phone tricks. Kurtz writes, "It is the considered judgment of Committee investigators that it is impossible to distinguish between what occurred at the Resch house and a simple hoax. Indeed, the Columbus 'poltergeist' may well turn out to be a classic case of media misinformation and public gullibility provoked in large measure by an adolescent with serious behavioral problems."

William Roll, however, argues that the case is proof of poltergeists. Roll acknowledges that of the poltergeist cases he has investigated, at least a third prove to have natural causes or direct evidence of trickery. He states, "I have observed Tina closely and I don't believe her claims are in any way part of a hoax." Roll feels that this case was the product of RSPK and that Tina was indeed the focus person of that energy.

James Randi concludes just the opposite. "The evidence for the validity of poltergeist claims in this case is anecdotal and thin, at best. The evidence against them is, in my estimation, strong and convincing."

Six

The Miami Poltergeist: Mystery or Mischief?

The poltergeist that plagued a Miami novelty supply warehouse for several months in 1966-67 quickly wore out its welcome. This unseen prankster attracted dozens of reporters, police officers, and curiosity seekers during its destructive visit to the warehouse. But the warehouse owners were soon disgusted at the cost.

The poltergeist's invasion began in mid-December, 1966, when Alvin Laubheim, part-owner of Tropication Arts, noticed a tremendous increase in breakage. At first Laubheim thought that his two shipping clerks, Julio Vasquez and Curt Hagemayer, were being unusually careless in handling breakable items. He warned them to be careful.

But the breakages continued. Glass beer mugs crashed to the floor. Boxes of pencil sharpeners spilled. Cartons of beach balls dropped off shelves. Boxes floated between shelves. Ashtrays smashed on the concrete floor.

On January 12, 1967, nearly a month after the strange events began, Laubheim showed Julio Vasquez exactly how to place the beer mugs on the shelves. He said, "Now, if you put them in this position, they are not going to break or fall off the shelf." Then, just as Laubheim turned away, one of the mugs crashed to the floor.

Laubheim recalls what happened next. "From then on, everything started to happen; boxes came down, a box of about a hundred back scratchers turned over and fell with a terrific clatter over on the other side of the room, and then we realized that there was something definitely wrong around here."

Laubheim decided to keep quiet about the mysterious destruction in the warehouse, but the poltergeist went on dropping, smashing, and spilling things.

Glen Lewis, Laubheim's partner, had not observed anything unusual until Friday the 13th. He came to the warehouse to help organize the shelves. He left convinced that a mischievous disorganizer was at work.

—"" *I don't believe in ghosts, but something is making a shambles of our warehouse."*

Tropicana Arts warehouse owner Alvin Laubheim

According to Lewis, this is what happened that afternoon: "I was skeptical when they told me about it over the phone, but when I was here and saw things being dropped off shelves right after I had placed them securely, then I knew something was mysterious about the whole thing. Different ashtrays, tumblers, jiggers, dropped, broke. Some of the burnt leather packages fell off the shelves mysteriously. I would put them back and they would continue to fall off the shelves."

Lewis asked his friend Howard Brooks, a magician, to help discover what sort of tricks were being played in the warehouse. Brooks said, "I discounted the whole thing. As a matter of fact, I made a practical joke of it by showing them how. While I was standing talking to someone, I took an article from behind my back and threw it. They all jumped

> **❝** *I can make things crash from shelves, too, when nobody is near them. Just a little piece of string and some spirit gum will do it easily. Or some dry ice. Any magician can do this."*
> Magician Howard Brooks

and said, 'There it goes again,' . . . so I wasn't convinced."

Two days later, however, Brooks was at the warehouse when two cartons dropped to the floor. Brooks could find no clues as to what caused it. He said, "I can't buy this spook theory at this point, but something did move those, and I couldn't figure out what."

Lewis and Laubheim called the police.

On January 14, Patrolman William Killin came to the warehouse. He suspected that the reported "ghost" was a hoax. However, he quickly became convinced of something

Magician Howard Brooks demonstrated how "poltergeist" activity might have been staged.

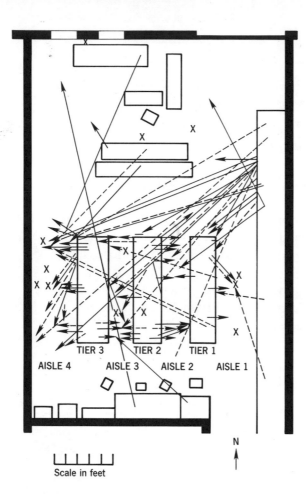

Floor plan of the Tropicana Arts warehouse showing the paths of many of the objects that were mysteriously thrown around.

TIER 3   TIER 2   TIER 1

AISLE 4   AISLE 3   AISLE 2   AISLE 1

N

Scale in feet

unusual when a glass shattered near him. He checked to see if anyone was near enough to have thrown it. No one was even close. He examined the glass for evidence of trickery but found nothing. He searched the shelves for clues but came up empty handed.

Still not entirely convinced that it wasn't trickery, Patrolman Killin questioned the employees. But when four

> **"** *Surely behind so much destructiveness must lie deep-seated aggressive urges, finding, we know not how, an outlet in these bizarre phenomena."*
> *Psychical investigators Alan Gauld and A.D. Cornell,* Poltergeists

other objects leapt from the shelves, Killin called for extra help.

Two patrolmen and a police sergeant soon arrived at the warehouse. The poltergeist became sneaky. It waited until the police were watching one area, then created a disturbance in another. The policemen were never quite certain that someone might not have thrown objects when their attention was diverted elsewhere. They left unconvinced of the existence of the ghost, but still wondering what was causing the breakages.

More Investigating

Two of the policemen continued investigating. They checked all the neighboring businesses to see if anyone else was having similar problems. No one was. They checked to see if sonic booms could have caused the shelves to move but found the shelves absolutely solid. They searched for evidence of underground gas accumulation or water currents

Boxes of beach balls mysteriously fell off the warehouse shelves.

Reporter Suzy Smith carefully observed Julio and the other warehouse workers. There seemed to be no explanation for items flying off the shelves.

or other natural causes, but found nothing.

By this time, the press had gotten word of the poltergeist and flocked to the warehouse to catch the ghost in action. TV crews, reporters, and writers hurried to Tropication Arts. One writer, Suzy Smith, was involved in the case for nearly a month and later wrote about it extensively in her book *Prominent American Ghosts*. Smith had written about numerous other ghost experiences and was considered an expert on American ghosts.

The poltergeist went into action soon after Smith arrived. Four boxes of beach balls weighing almost nine pounds moved on their shelf when no one was near them.

Smith wasn't convinced that anything mysterious had actually happened.

"Still I remained skeptical," she wrote. "I had to observe one of these moving objects myself."

The poltergeist gave her what she wanted. Within moments, a box of fans fell to the floor and spilled. Smith

Julio Vasquez and reporter Suzy Smith.

checked the shelf but found no evidence of trickery. "I could see nothing there to account for the activity," she wrote.

Had someone tricked Smith by throwing the box and quickly hiding? Smith wondered if this might be true. So she set up an experiment.

That afternoon when Glen Lewis, Curt Hagemayer, and Julio Vasquez were arranging things on the shelves, Smith sat in a position where she could watch all three. If anyone threw something, she would certainly witness it.

Yet as she observed the three men, a box of rubber daggers fell in another aisle of the warehouse. While the four were investigating this event, a china sailfish ashtray crashed to the floor some twenty-five feet away.

No Evidence of Tricks

Still Smith was unconvinced. She wrote, "When I had to leave soon afterward, it was with the conviction that something unusual was definitely afoot at Tropication Arts. Yet I argued with myself constantly as soon as I left the shop, certain that there was some clue I had overlooked. Perhaps there was some kind of trigger I didn't know about, like a rubber band which would snap back and remain unseen on the shelf after causing a box to fall. Or dry ice against which a dish could have been tilted until the ice melted and threw the dish off balance and onto the floor."

But the next day Smith could find no evidence of such trick devices. "We shook the shelves often, and proved to ourselves that objects could not be shaken off them, nor could they be blown off by the large and powerful electric fan, and they could hardly even be nudged off by a careless elbow."

Stumped, Smith called William Roll, the psychic investigator from the Psychical Research Foundation. Roll began his investigation of the Miami poltergeist on January 19. He was disappointed at first. The poltergeist would not perform.

❝ *He [a Miami detective] insisted that he had solved the entire case of the spook in the stockroom by extracting from a 'sick' youth employed there the confession that it had all been done with a network of threads, which had been cleverly manipulated when no one was looking."*

Author *Suzy Smith,* Prominent American Ghosts

Roll commented on this in his book *The Poltergeist.* "In some of my other investigations, the phenomena seemed to decrease or stop when I arrived. It is natural to suspect that this was because somebody was causing the incidents by trickery and that he was afraid to continue when he thought he was being watched. However, the police and others who had investigated the occurrences in the warehouse before I came, did not jinx the poltergeist."

Roll left the warehouse to see if the poltergeist would become active in his absence. The magician Howard Brooks stayed behind to keep an eye on things. Within ten minutes of Roll's departure, a beer mug crashed to the floor.

Roll decided to study this poltergeist by experimentation. He would keep in the background during his experiments and let things happen. He established strict criteria for his experiments. First he set up a target area, which had been thoroughly checked beforehand to eliminate the possibility of magical devices, loose boards, chemicals, or other tricks. A target object, which had also been thoroughly examined, was then put in the target area. If a target object moved, the observer could document its movement, calculate how far it had moved, and immediately investigate for any evidence of trickery.

Roll asked his colleague Gaither Pratt, another parapsychologist, to help him. Pratt, whose identity was kept secret to fool any tricksters, kept watch when Roll left the warehouse.

The poltergeist cooperated several times, once by breaking a target object, a ceramic spoon-drip tray, while Pratt was observing. Pratt reported, "During the period preceding this event I was observing the activity in the room

Did Julio Vasquez cause the poltergeist events because he was angry with his bosses?

and recording a running description of the situation on tape from my position in the southwest corner of the room. This record continued right up to the instant when the tray fell and broke. The point on the shelf where it was standing was not visible from my observation point. I could, however, see Julio. I could see both of his hands. In one he held a clipboard, and the other was by his side. At the time of the incident he was walking toward my position. No one was in Aisle 2 where the tray fell and broke, and Julio was the nearest person. I was not able to conceive of any way in which the falling of the tray could have been caused to happen in a normal manner."

Altogether Pratt and Roll identified 224 mysterious breakages at the warehouse. Some had happened before they became involved, many after they began their investigation.

As the investigation continued it became evident that Julio Vasquez was the focus person at the warehouse. The events occurred only when Julio was at work. Julio was nineteen at the time and was frustrated with his work. He did not like Al Laubheim. After Laubheim shouted at Curt Hagemayer, Julio told an investigator, "That's no way to talk to a man." Julio had been treated similarly and was clearly frustrated that he could not complain as it would cost him his job.

Did he cause the tricks for revenge? Although no direct evidence was collected that proved Julio's guilt, a motive was clearly there.

Investigation of the poltergeist phenomena at the warehouse ended in late January. Suspected of theft, Julio was fired. Remarkably, the poltergeist events stopped, too.

Laboratory Experiments

Were the poltergeist phenomena examples of RSPK with Julio's deep frustrations releasing the energy to move objects? To answer this question Roll invited Julio to the laboratory at the Psychical Research Foundation in Durham.

There Julio was given a number of psychological tests to discover facets of his personality. Dr. John Altrocchi tested Julio and found evidence of "anger, rebellion, a feeling of not being part of the social environment, a feeling that he doesn't get what is coming to him and lack of strongly

pleasant experiences in life."

Julio apparently did get great pleasure out of the poltergeist phenomena at the warehouse. When questioned about the events he even said, "I feel happy. That thing [the breakage of an ashtray] makes me feel happy; I don't know why." Later, when nothing unusual happened for a while, Julio said, "Now I am nervous when nothing happens." Then when four incidents happened in quick succession Julio told William Roll, "I feel good. I really miss the ghost . . . I mean, not the ghost, but I miss it when nothing happens."

Julio was also tested for ESP and PK ability. The results were inconclusive.

Roll claims that Julio did accomplish a first in the parapsychology lab: Julio created a genuine poltergeist event.

During the second night of testing, Roll and several other investigators were taking a break and Julio was drinking a cup of coffee. Suddenly a large vase fell from a table sixteen feet from Julio and moved towards him. None of the investigators found any strings or other suspicious devices which might have caused the vase to fall. The only explanation, Roll believed, was that the vase was moved by a poltergeist caused by a release of PK energy by Julio.

A Genuine Case?

Gaither Pratt wrote, "I have no doubt in my mind that [the Miami poltergeist] was a genuine case. There's no room for doubt in view of the circumstances under which we were able to make our observations."

Yet Roll admits that one of the key proofs of a poltergeist, seeing an object actually leave its resting place, was missing in this case. "In one respect," Roll writes, "Gaither and I were disappointed in the Miami poltergeist. Neither of us ever saw an object begin its movement."

Skeptic James Randi raises an interesting point about poltergeist investigations and their parapsychologist investigators. He states that "the major difference between the skeptic and the parapsychologist is one of expectation." Did the investigators of the Miami poltergeist come to Miami expecting to have their theories about poltergeists proven? If they expected to find a poltergeist, might they indeed have "found" him? Was Julio able to trick them into believing what they wanted to believe?

Other questions remain regarding the Miami poltergeist. These shed considerable doubt on the evidence. Why were other scientists not called in to investigate? Why were only poltergeist believers involved in this case? Why was Julio unable to demonstrate any PK or RSPK ability repeatedly in the lab? Why did the events suddenly stop when Julio was fired?

The Search
for Truth
Goes On

The Miami case highlights one of the prime difficulties in proving the existence of poltergeists—that *skeptical* investigators are often not involved in investigating or are kept away from firsthand involvement, as in the Columbus case.

Such onesidedness is common in questions of the paranormal. One reason is the public's continual interest in the mysterious. Events are hastily reported to satisfy public curiosity. Premature reports often give the impression of being factual, and the public believes them. Only certain aspects of an event may have been examined, yet they are presented as proof of the unknown.

Much remains to be proven in regard to the existence of poltergeists. Claims of real poltergeist phenomena seem at times to be established. Yet questions arise about the validity and reliability of witnesses. Evidence of fraud is often

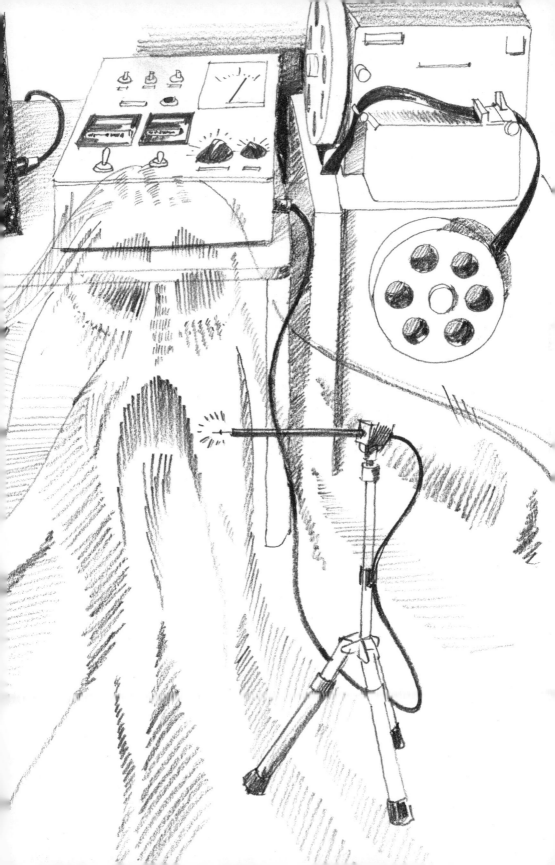

shown. Yet not all of the events can be explained in this way.

The belief in these unique ghosts continues. Until someone can trap a poltergeist and test it under laboratory conditions—conditions that demonstrate beyond doubt that poltergeists are real creatures or real events caused by a focus person—the mystery will remain. Until it is solved, scientific investigation should continue.

Books for Further Exploration

Peter and Connie Roop recommend the following books:

Jean Bendick, *Scare a Ghost, Tame a Monster.* Philadelphia: The Westminster Press, 1983.

Norma Bowles and Fran Hynds, *Psi Search.* New York: Harper & Row, 1978.

Daniel Cohen, *In Search of Ghosts.* New York: Dodd, Mead, & Co., 1972.

Jose Feola, *Mind Over Matter.* Minneapolis: Dillon Press, 1975.

Larry Kettlekamp, *Haunted Houses.* New York: William Morrow, 1969.

Joseph Gaither Pratt, *Parapsychology: An Insider's View of ESP.* New York: E.P. Dutton & Co., 1966.

James Randi, *Flim-Flam!* Buffalo, NY: Prometheus Books, 1982.

William G. Roll, *The Poltergeist.* Metuchen, NJ: The Scarecrow Press, 1986.

Suzy Smith, *Prominent American Ghosts.* New York: World Publishing Co., 1967.

Gurney Williams III, *Ghosts and Poltergeists.* New York: Franklin Watts, 1979.

Colin Wilson, *Poltergeist.* New York: G.P. Putnam, 1981.

Glossary

focus person person around whom the poltergeist activity seems to concentrate; usually boys and girls in puberty

paranormal phenomenon an event which cannot be explained scientifically

parapsychologist researcher into scientifically unexplained events such as poltergeists, ghosts, levitation, and ESP

phenomenon an event

poltergeist a "noisy ghost" which sometimes moves things

psychokinesis also called **PK**; the ability to move things with mind-controlled energy

recurrent spontaneous psychokinesis also called **RSPK**; repeated psychokinetic events which seem to be uncontrolled

skeptic one who questions and doubts

More Poltergeists!!

Tales of poltergeists have been reported all over the world. Here are a few more of these fascinating stories. Do you think they are truth or fiction?

Tedworth, England, 1661

William Drury, a vagrant, was arrested for noise pollution! He was accused of being a nuisance—of beating a drum loudly and disturbing the peace. Judge Mompesson had him put in jail and took away his drum. Drury escaped, but he was unable to get his drum back.

The drum was sent to Judge Mompesson's home while the judge was out of town. When he returned home, he found his household completely upset. For three nights there had been violent taps and drumming noises throughout the house. The night the judge returned, the noises started again. Mompesson, gun in hand, leaped out of bed and ran around the house trying to find the location of the noise. He couldn't find the source, but he *could* hear drumbeats.

The loud and annoying drumming went on every night for at least two hours. It continued for two months, stopped for a few weeks during and after the birth of a baby, and then started again, this time focusing on the Mompesson children. The drumbeats came from around their beds, and their beds were sometimes lifted up into the air. Was this a poltergeist at work?

The incidents increased. Over the next two years, strange lights came and went, doors opened and closed, and people and animals were attacked. Mompesson's horse died a mysterious death; guests had items snatched from their hands; garbage was dumped into the children's beds.

In 1663, William Drury was arrested again in another town. While in jail, he claimed to be the cause of the strange circumstances in Tedworth. He claimed that he was doing these things because his drum had been taken from him. He was tried for witchcraft but found innocent. Sentenced for another crime, he was deported from England. Again, he escaped his sentence and returned. The bizarre events in the Mompesson household began again.

History does not record how this case was resolved. Was William Drury able to cause the events? Was it a poltergeist? Or was there some other explanation?

Tennessee, USA, 1817

John Bell, his wife, and five of his children lived on a pleasant farm tended with the help of a few slaves. One day the family began hearing odd noises—rappings and scratchings which gradually became louder and louder. Soon even stranger things began to happen. Bed covers were mysteriously pulled off in the middle of the night, and family members were "slapped" by an invisible hand. John Bell was unusually affected, frequently feeling as though his tongue were so swollen with a mysterious "fungus" that he couldn't speak.

Often the mysterious force seemed most interested in the daughter Betsy, twelve years old when the poltergeist first began its work. It slapped her and pulled her hair. Eventually, when a young man said he wanted to marry her, the poltergeist did all kinds of things to break up the couple.

The family asked a friend and neighbor, a popular amateur preacher, to help them. The preacher and a group of people he gathered investigated the Bell farm thoroughly. They could find no cause for the strange events.

Gradually, the poltergeist began to try to communicate. First it made unusual whistling noises that sounded a little like words; soon it was able to talk in a soft whispery voice; gradually it was able to be fully understood. It would answer questions when it felt like it. Sometimes it would shriek and howl.

The poltergeist, which people called the Bell Witch, told its listeners many different things about itself. Once it said it was a mysterious spirit from "everywhere." Another time it said it was the spirit of a murdered man whose bones and teeth had been scattered around the farm. On still another occasion it claimed to be the spirit of an old woman who was still living on a nearby farm.

For a reason no one ever knew, the poltergeist claimed to hate John Bell. It pursued him, tricked him, and tried many ways to make him miserable. The poltergeist persisted with its tricks for three years. Slowly John Bell's health declined. One day he fell into a coma. The poltergeist cackled and said it had poisoned him. A smoky brown bottle of liquid that no one had even seen before was found in a cupboard. When a drop of it was given to a cat, the cat died. John Bell died the next day.

After John Bell's death, the poltergeist's activities slowed down. However, several months after the funeral, the poltergeist made a final dramatic appearance. Out of a mysterious burst of smoke, the poltergeist's voice said it was leaving but would return in seven years.

Seven years later, several members of the family still lived in the home. Sure enough, strange noises began and bed covers flew off again. This time, the events never became more serious and ended after only a few weeks. One family member said he heard the poltergeist's voice say that it would return again in one hundred and seven years, but that did not happen.

Sumatra, 1906

A Dutch traveler, W.G. Grottendieck, experienced a poltergeist one night in the jungle. He had settled for the evening in a hut made of branches and roofed with leaves. His only companion was a native boy who was his servant.

In the middle of the night, he was startled awake by the sound of something hitting the floor near his head. He saw that it was a black stone and that other stones were falling around him, apparently from nowhere. He lit his lamp and sent the boy outside to see if the stones were being thrown from the jungle. The boy found nothing. He and the boy examined the inside of the hut carefully. They found no signs of another person or of an animal that could be throwing the stones.

As the stones continued to fall, Mr. Grottendieck tried to catch one of them. Although they seemed to be falling slowly, he couldn't grasp even one. It was as if they changed direction when his hands came near.

Still puzzled and annoyed, he and the boy climbed up the walls and examined the roof. Again they could find no cause and no source of the mysterious falling stones. By morning, they stopped, and the rest of Mr. Grottendieck's journey was uneventful. Had it been a jungle poltergeist that threw the stones?

Long Island, USA, 1958

The normal lives of Mr. and Mrs. James Herrmann and their two children, thirteen-year-old Lucille and twelve-year-old Jimmy, was shattered when a poltergeist began to haunt their home. On February 11, with no warning, bottles began loudly popping their caps; others spilled their contents of holy water, household cleansers, and medicines; untouched toys broke. The Herrmanns were alarmed but at first assumed there must have been some unusual earth tremors or another natural cause. When the unexplained happenings continued for several days, Mrs. Herrmann called the police.

The police investigated thoroughly. They even witnessed incidents of bottles and other objects moving, falling, breaking, and spilling. But they could find no reason for the disturbances.

Investigators from the Parapsychology Laboratory at Duke

University went to the Herrmann home. During the ten days they were there, they witnessed several events of thumpings and unexplained movement of furniture, bottles, and other objects.

After interviewing all the people who had been in the home during the incidents, the investigators could detect no sign of fraud. They searched for possible mechanical sources of the disturbances. They checked for underground water channels and electrical malfunctions. But they found nothing that could explain the mysterious activities. They attempted to reproduce the events and were able to recreate some of them. But they were unable to do any of them in such a way that it wouldn't be obvious to any witness what was going on. The only important discovery was that the events occurred only when Jimmy was home. They questioned him in great detail, but Jimmy appeared upset and claimed that he was innocent. The investigators found nothing to contradict that.

Mysteriously, the events ended a few weeks after they began. No explanation was ever found.

Bremen, Germany, 1968

A German china shop was once the victim of a lively poltergeist. For a period of time, figurines, vases, glasses, and other fragile objects were violently thrown to the floor by an invisible force. The police investigated but could find no cause for the extensive breakage.

Someone familiar with poltergeists' seeming attraction to young people suggested that the fifteen-year-old apprentice, Heiner, be sent away. When he left, so did the poltergeist.

Professor Hans Bender heard about the events and decided to investigate. He discovered that Heiner was a very unhappy boy. Professor Bender learned that when Heiner first began working at the china shop, he had broken an abnormally large number of items. His family, thinking he must be disturbed, had sent him to a psychological laboratory for tests. This had distressed him even more. As soon as he had returned to his job, new, unexplained breakage began, but no one could catch Heiner breaking items. No evidence was found of trickery by Heiner—no signs of secret strings or other devices to pull glasses over. Yet the china shop continued to suffer.

After Heiner was fired from his job, Professor Bender arranged to examine him. While under Bender's scrutiny, Heiner took a job as apprentice to an electrician. Bizarre things began to happen on this job also.

Part of the job was to drill holes in walls and insert plastic plugs and screws. But when Heiner was around, screws would loosen and fall out of the wall. Professor Bender's crew tried some experiments.

They installed two hooks into a wall, fastening each with two screws. Then they tested the screws to make sure that they were tight. When they were done, they asked Heiner to stand about two feet from the wall. Carefully they watched Heiner and the wall. Suddenly the screws became loose and the hooks fell off the wall. Heiner had not moved.

Bender did ESP and PK tests on Heiner. The PK tests didn't show anything, but Heiner had unusually high scores on the ESP tests.

After a few weeks, the poltergeist activities slowed down. But Heiner tried to keep them going by using tricks. Although these tricks were detected, they raised questions about the other, unexplained events. Was Heiner the focus of a genuine poltergeist or not?

Wisconsin, USA, 1983

Tim and Louise Mulderink were the new owners of an old house they had remodeled and turned into a restaurant. One day, Louise was standing near the bar when a glass exploded. No one was near the glass, and no other glasses on the shelf broke.

A little later another glass, filled with a drink, exploded in front of the customer who had ordered it. Over the next several days, more glasses shattered. Finally, Tim talked to the person who had sold them the glasses. The salesman said that occasionally a glass will shatter, but it was highly unlikely that several glasses would.

Soon more strange things began to happen. The heavy front door began to open by itself. Even when the restaurant was closed for the night, the locked door would open. This was witnessed at different times by several people who happened to be working in the house alone. Next, the bar clock began striking thirteen instead of midnight. Other unusual sounds and movements occurred.

One night when Louise was working alone, she heard a door open and close and footsteps in another room. She went to investigate but found no sign of another living person. Then she heard a musical tinkling and saw the metal hangers on the coat rack moving as though someone had brushed by them.

Many nights the lights in the building would be seen burning even though they had been carefully turned off before the last person went home.

The Mulderinks investigated many possible causes. There were no strong breezes to blow the doors open. There were no earth tremors. They researched the background of the house and found that some of the previous owners had been very religious people who did not believe in drinking. Is it possible that a spirit from the past was making gentle objections to having its home turned into a restaurant?

Thousands of Poltergeists?

These are only a few of the thousands of poltergeist events that have been reported. You can read about more of them in the books listed on page 83 or in others at your library.

Index

Illustration Credits

About the Authors

Peter and Connie Roop majored in geology at Lawrence University in Appleton, Wisconsin. Peter, an elementary school teacher, writes historical articles and stories. In 1986 he was named Wisconsin Teacher of the Year. Connie, a junior high science teacher, serves as a science specialist for *Appraisal* magazine and writes for educational journals. They earned their Masters degrees in Boston and have taught in England.

The Roops have co-authored a dozen books for young people, including *Keep the Lights Burning, Abbie* which was featured on public television's *Reading Rainbow*. They are the authors of three Great Mysteries: Opposing Viewpoints—*Dinosaurs, Poltergeists,* and *The Solar System.*

Peter and Connie live in Appleton, Wisconsin with their children Sterling and Heidi with whom they enjoy traveling, camping, and reading.